Origami

Easy Step-by-step Origami Guide for Kids

Copyright © 2020

All rights reserved.

DEDICATION

Contents

Modular Origami Cube Box 1

Origami Finger Puppets 5

Traditional Floating Origami Boat 12

Origami Fortune Teller 16

Easy Origami Puppy Face 24

Easy Origami House 29

Easy Origami Butterfly 34

Elephant Corner Bookmark.................................40

Basic Paper Airplane 48

Modular Origami Cube Box

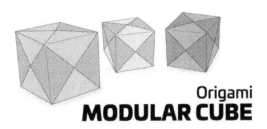

Beginning Folds

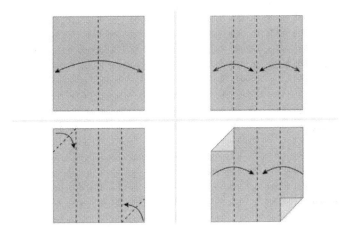

Start with your paper white side up if it has one.

1. Fold your paper in half from left to right and unfold. You now

have a central crease.

2. Fold the left and right edges to the central crease and unfold.

3. Fold the top left corner and bottom right corner inwards, aligning with the two previous creases.

4. Fold the left and right edges back to the central crease.

Make Diagonal Folds, Rotate, and Repeat

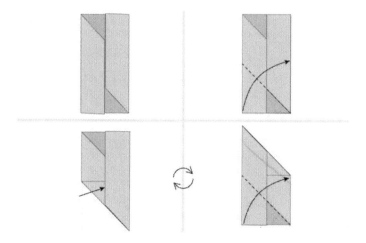

1. Fold the lower-left section diagonally up to the right along the diagonal flap that is in the right section.

2. Tuck the flap you just created underneath the right section.

3. Rotate the paper and fold the lower-left corner up in the same way as before.

Connect Your Sonobe Units

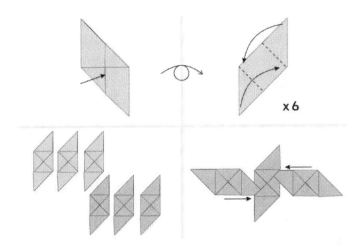

1. Insert the flap underneath the lower right section.

2. Flip the model over to the other side, left to right.

3. Fold the lower-left corner up to the lower point of the right edge.

4. Fold the topmost point down and to the left.

5. You now need to have six of these "Sonobe" units.

6. Start by taking one unit with its flap on the top and bottom. Then take two more, place them on the left and right of the first one. The two on either side have their flaps out to the right and left.

The left one: Insert the bottom right point into the bottom pocket of the center unit.

The right one: Insert the top left point into the top pocket on the center unit.

Finishing Up

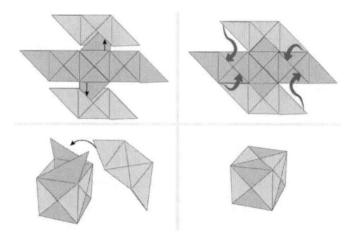

1. Now get two more Sonobe units, place them above and below the central unit.

2. Insert the top flap from the central unit into the right pocket of the one above.

3. Insert the bottom flap from the central unit into the left pocket of the one below.

4. Now it's time to pick up the units, but be care full they don't all come apart. Shape the units into a box, inserting the flaps as shown.

5. Now that you have a box, you can get the last unit and finish the origami cube.

Origami Finger Puppets

This origami model is a Traditional design. For this finger puppet, it would be nice to use paper that has a white side and a colored side, but if not, your puppet will still work fine!

The paper needs to be square, so ensure you have the right type of paper on hand.

This origami puppet looks like a cute cat, but you can make other animal faces too, such as a bat or dog, by drawing a different face, or folding the ears differently. For a fun craft activity for kids, you can decorate these with glitter, sequins, and ribbons!

Origami Finger Puppet Tutorial - Step 1

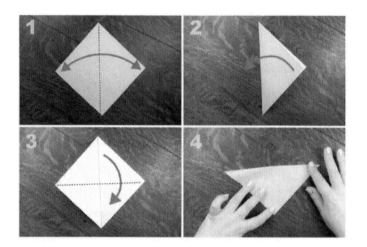

Start white side up.

1. Fold in half vertically.

2. Unfold.

3. Fold in half horizontally.

Origami Finger Puppet Tutorial - Step 2

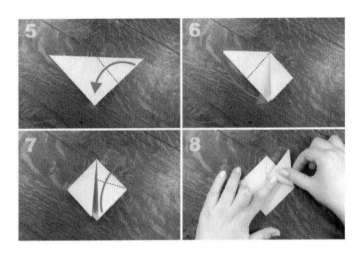

5. Fold the right corner down to the bottom center point.

6. Fold the left corner down to the bottom center point.

7. Fold the right flap up from the center as shown.

8. Roughly position the flap with the right edge at a 90-degree angle.

Origami Finger Puppet Tutorial - Step 3

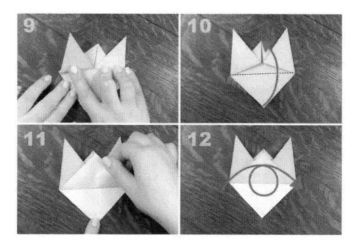

9. Fold the left flap in the same way as the right.

10 & 11. Fold one layer from the bottom section up to the top point.

12. Turn the model over.

Origami Finger Puppet Tutorial - Step 4

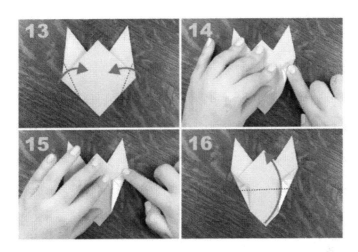

13. Fold the left and right edges inwards as shown in #14 & 15.

16. Fold the bottom section up to the top point.

Origami Finger Puppet Tutorial - Step 5

17 - 19. Fold the top section down, including all layers.

You could stick these down if you like.

20. Turn the model over.

Origami Finger Puppet Tutorial - Step 6

21 & 22. Draw a cute face!

Your cute little finger puppet it finished!

Don't worry if it didn't work out the first time, just try again, it can take practice.

Traditional Floating Origami Boat

Origami comes from the Japanese. The word means the art of folding paper. "Ori" means "folding," and kami means "paper." In modern usage, the word "origami" is used as an inclusive term for all folding practices. The goal is to transform a flat square sheet of paper into a finished sculpture through folding and sculpting techniques.

Learn how to make the most well-known origami boat with this quick and easy step-by-step tutorial. This origami boat can also float in water.

This origami boat is a great model to teach kids. It is similar to the origami hat that you make with newspaper. Also, origami can be a great math-related activity for kids as your child creates using geometry.

What You'll Need

1 Rectangular sheet of paper

Instructions

1. Make the First Folds

Start with your rectangular paper, orient it vertically, with the long edges going up and down. Fold the bottom half up to the top. Fold the bottom right corner over to the left corner and make a small pinch, just enough to crease the paper. Open it back up.

2. Create a Triangle Shape

Using the crease as a guide, fold the left and right bottom corners up and to the middle. Flatten the folded pieces down. Rotate the paper. Fold one layer from the bottom up along the bottom of the front flaps.

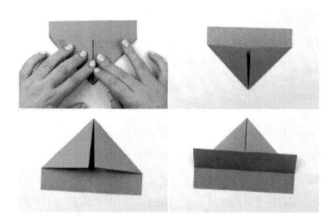

3. A Boat Begins to Take Shape

Flip the paper over to the other side. Fold the bottom edge up in the same way. Unfold, and then fold the bottom right corner in along the crease you made. Repeat on the bottom left flap.

4. Form the Bottom of the Boat

Re-fold the bottom edge back up. Open the bottom of the model.

Look at the corners. Flatten and then insert the overlapping flap on the left underneath the right section.

5. Continue Folding

Fold one layer up to the top. Repeat on the back. Open the bottom of the model.

6. Finalize the Folds

Pull apart the left and right flaps. Flatten it out, in the shape of a boat. Open it slightly. The triangle in the middle resembles a sail.

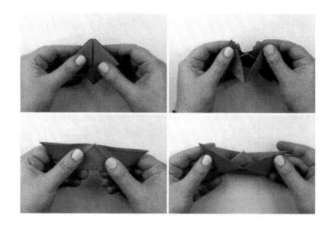

Origami Fortune Teller

Learn how to make an Origami Cootie Catcher. These fun origami fortune tellers are easy to make and simple to play with! Follow this step by step tutorial to find out how!

If you grew up in the 90s it's likely that you remember folding these origami fortune tellers at school!

Follow this photo tutorial to refresh your memory or learn from scratch if this trend missed you! You will need one sheet of square paper, any paper will do, printer paper is perfect.

Beginning Folds

Start with your paper with its white side facing up (if you have one!).

1. Start by folding your square sheet of paper in half diagonally both ways, ending up with a nice X.

2. Fold all four corners neatly to the central point of the X. Crease well!

3. Flip the paper over to the other side.

4. Fold all four corners to the central point!

18

Keep Folding

1. Fold the paper in half, top to bottom, unfold and fold in half from left to right and unfold.

2. Pick up the paper.

3. Start to push all the points inwards.

4. Use your fingers to pinch the paper to the center.

Finishing Folds

1. Rotate the paper to the side and pull out the flaps!
2. After a bit of shaping, your origami fortune teller is made!
3. You can make sure your origami cootie catcher has good movement by opening and closing it back and forth.

How to Decorate It for the Cootie Catcher Game

Now we need to prepare the fortune teller! Have your cootie catcher flattened and with the outer flaps facing up.

1. Get a pen and write four words, they don't have to be colors. Alternatively, they could be drawings of animals, such as fish, cat, horse, elephant.

2. Flip the paper over, and write the numbers 1 through 8 on each of the sections.

3. Open out the flaps you drew the numbers on. You can write your 'fortunes' in these sections.

4. In the example, we have used simple outcomes such as 'yes', 'no' and 'maybe'. You can make these answers more elaborate, or more specific to your situation!

5. You can also use the upper sections for the answers!

How to Play the Cootie Catcher Game

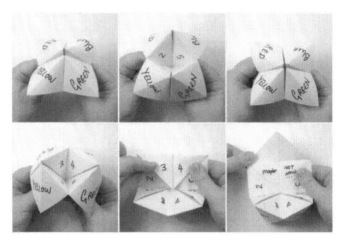

1. Reasemble the fortune teller, and hold it out, closed, to your friend (or yourself!).

2. Have them pick a color (or whatever words you used).

3. You will now count open and close the fortune teller, and alternate the direction you open it.

4. Open and close the fortune teller as many times as there are letters in the word.

5. Hold the fortune teller open at the end of your counting.

6. Next, show it to your friend and ask them to choose a number.

7. Again open and close the fortune teller, as many times as the number they chose.

8. Hold out the fortune teller again, asking them to chose a second number.

9. Open out the paper, and the answer is under the number they chose.

To take it a step further, if you have different answers on the upper and lower sections you can ask them 'up or down?' and read the answer from either the top or bottom section.

Easy Origami Puppy Face

The art of paper folding is known as origami. It's a great inexpensive craft to make with children because all you need is paper! This pattern is a good example of how you can take most traditional origami models further to make them unique. Add extra folds at the end or slightly adjust angles to produce a different head or ear shapes.

The traditional origami dog face is usually made without the nose, tongue, or lower jaw. If you had a paper that is white on one side, though, you could easily draw on the tongue and muzzle color.

You just need one sheet of square paper for this. To start with, the suggested paper size is at least 15 by 15 centimeters. The more comfortable you get with origami, the smaller you can go.

For other very simple origami models, try the loopy origami paper plane diagram, easy origami card stand tutorial, or easy traditional origami turtle instructions.

Start in a Dimond Position

1. Start white side up. Place the paper in a diamond position.
2. Fold the top corner down to the bottom.
3. Fold the right corner over to the left.
4. Unfold one side.

Folding the Puppy Face

1. Fold one corner down, leaving a small gap at the top of the middle crease.

2. Fold the other side down to match.

3. You can now fold the bottom corner up and behind. You can finish here for the simplest origami dog face. To make either the puppy's tongue or lower jaw, fold one layer of the bottom up and continue to the next step.

Folding the Puppy Jaw

1. Fold the flap back down again to meet the bottom of the head.

2. Flip the model over to the other side.

3. Fold the lower flap down, leaving a small gap.

4. Fold the bottom corner up a tiny bit to round out the tongue and jaw.

5. If this is to be the jaw, it's finished. Continue to the next step if you're making a tongue.

Make the Puppy Tounge

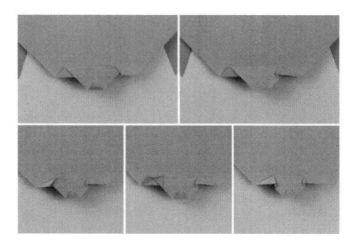

1. Fold the right corner of the lower section down as shown.
2. Unfold and use your finger to bring the flap out and over to the left.
3. Repeat on the left side.
4. This line is where the fold will be. Doesn't matter if it doesn't look neat.

If these steps are too tricky for you, simply use some scissors to snip the shape of the tongue.

Easy Origami House

easy origami house

Learn how to make a super simple origami house with these easy to follow step by step instructions. This origami house is perfect for kids to fold. Kids age 4 or older will have no problem with this model, it's so simple.

You can add your own window and door like we did or leave it as it is, you can also turn it upside down, and use it as a boat too.

For this quick origami house, you'll just need one sheet of square paper. The paper we used is 15 x 15 cm and has two colors, but you can use any kind of paper you like.

First Set of Steps

- Start with the paper with the color you'd like on the roof, facing down. (My house will have an orange roof).

- Fold the paper in half, and unfold.

- Fold the top edge of the paper down to the crease we just made in the middle.

- This is what you should have.

Second Set of Steps

1. Flip the paper over, left to right.

2. Fold the bottom edge up to the middle crease.

3. We will be making a small mark in the middle where indicated.

4. Bring the right edge over to the left and align.

5. Don't fold it all; make a small mark at the top.

Third Set of Steps

- You can see the little crease in the middle. We'll now be folding where it is indicated.
- Bring the right edge to the mark we just made in the middle. Only the fold the lower section (the blue part in my case).
- Pull the flap out to the right.
- You can now flatten that flap.

Fourth Set of Steps

- Repeat all of the steps on the left side.
- You can now flip the house over to the other side, and have a cute little origami house!

Why not draw a window, door or more decorations!

Easy Origami Butterfly

Using an easy-to-follow tutorial, you can learn how to make a little origami butterfly. It's a traditional origami model that is a good introduction to the art of paper folding popularized by the Japanese. The word origami means "folding paper" (ori means "folding," and kami is "paper" in Japanese).

The origami butterfly has a simple but elegant look. Once you learn how to make one, you won't want to stop. An entire group of paper butterflies makes a wonderful wall decoration. You can also use them to embellish handmade cards, scrapbooks, and even as the finishing touch on gift wrapping.

You will need one sheet of square paper for each origami butterfly. For a bold look, use solid colored paper. If you'd like an elegant and traditional Japanese look, try authentic washi paper. Washi paper is made in a traditional manner and processed by hand from fibers native to Japan. The fibers come from the inner bark of the gampi tree, the mitsumata shrub, or the paper mulberry bush.

You could also use other types of paper, such as newspaper, music sheets, or wrapping paper to make these if you do not have any fancy origami paper. You might want to practice on scrap paper until you get used to the folds so you don't waste the paper you intend to use for your project.

Tips

- As you fold the paper, make sure your folds are as crisp and clean as possible. Do not overdo the folding, though, because you don't want the paper to rip.
- If you have two-sided colored paper, start off with your paper white-side-up to ensure that your butterfly is colored when it is done.

What You'll Need

1 sheet square-shaped paper

Instructions

1. Get Started

Start by folding diagonally, both ways, and then old the paper in half, both ways. Fold all four corners into the center.

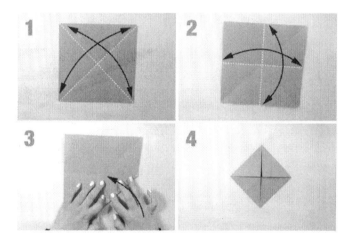

2. Flip Over

Flip the paper over, and fold all four corners into the center. Unfold the previous step and flip the model over to the other side. Unfold the paper.

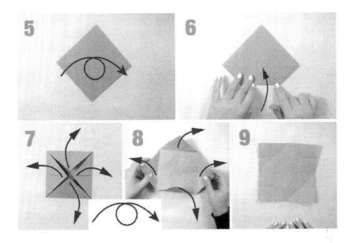

3. Get Ready to Make Flaps

Fold the right side into the center. Fold the left side to the center, too.

Holding the paper in the center, pull the right flap out to the right. Pull the left flap out in the same way, and flatten the top section.

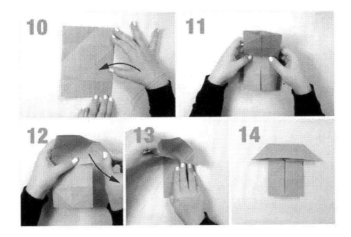

4. Make More Flaps

Make the same right and left flaps for the bottom section. Flatten what you have. It should look like a squat, rather horizontal hexagon.

Fold the top section behind. Flatten the model.

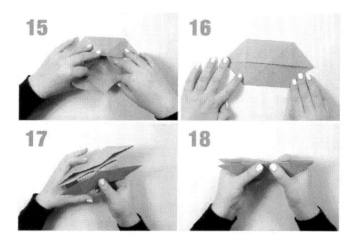

5. Fold It Into a Quarter of Its Size

Flip the right layer down. Flip the left flap down. Fold a small section inward where indicated. Fold the model in half to the right.

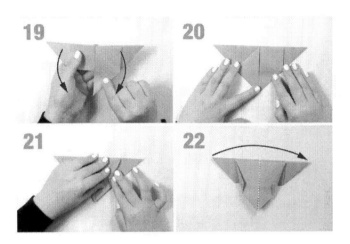

6. Finish Up

Fold a small section over where shown. Unfold the back layer to the left. Reverse fold the left side of the fold you just created.

Tip

If your butterfly did not come out like the illustration, just give it another go. The issue is usually that your folds are not as precise as you had hoped. Simply get new paper and start again and remember that origami becomes easier with practice

Elephant Corner Bookmark

What you need:

blue or gray origami paper

blue or gray paper

black marker

scissors

glue

wiggle eye stickers or googly eyes (optional)

Tutorial

1. Prepare a sheet of origami paper. We are using blue, but gray, violet (or well any other color) will work out just as great.

2. Fold the paper in half, with the white side on the inside, diagonally to get a triangle.

3. Fold one of the paper layers (grab the top of the triangle) towards the bottom.

4. A white square inside the triangle will show.

5. Now bring the right corner of the triangle to the bottom middle. Make the fold crisp and unfold.

6. Do the same with the other side.

7. Now take the same right corner only this time bring it to the top.

8. Repeat with the other corner (a diamond shape will form).

9. Tuck the tops into the "pocket". The corner bookmark is complete. Now let's turn it into an elephant bookmark.

10.   Cut two big ears out of the other sheet of paper.

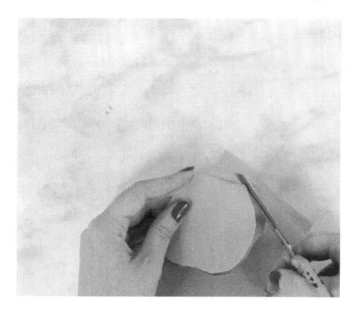

11.   You can make the ears symmetrical by first folding the

paper in half and cutting both ears simultaneously.

12.   Also cut the trunk (and if you want the tusks).

13.   Glue the trunk on the corner bookmark.

14.   Do the same with the ears.

15.   Now add details with a black marker.

16.   You can either draw the eyes with the marker or use

wiggle eye stickers or googly eyes.

17.   All done, the only thing left to do is to place it in your favorite book.

Basic Paper Airplane

This particular simple paper airplane works best with six-inch lightweight origami paper squares. Although many origami projects can be folded with scrapbook paper, magazine pages, calendar pages, and other types of materials, the origami airplane needs a lightweight paper to fly well. Thicker paper is also more difficult to fold, which makes it more likely that your plane will be asymmetrical and end up taking a quick nosedive when it's launched for the first time.

1. Make the Initial Folds

Start by folding a square piece of origami paper in half with the white side facing up. Crease well, then unfold. Turn and fold in half from the other direction. Crease well, then unfold.

Fold the top of your paper into the middle crease. When you're finished, your paper airplane should look like the photo to the left.

2. Fold the Corners Down

Fold the left corner down to meet the edge of the colored side of your paper. Fold the right corner in the same manner.

3. Make the Nose of Your Simple Paper Airplane

Fold the left and right corners of your origami paper in so your project resembles the photo at the left. The pointed end will be the nose of your origami airplane. The extra folds you made in the previous step help give the nose the additional weight it needs to make your simple paper airplane fly properly.

4. Fold Your Paper Along the Middle Crease

Fold your paper in half along the middle crease. Fold the right corner up as shown in the picture to the left. The corner should be about 1/2-inch from the edge of the paper. Unfold the paper, flip it over and fold it from the other direction along the same crease.

5. Make Your Airplane's Tail

Open your paper and collapse the fold you made in the previous step. If you're having trouble getting the fold to collapse, go over the creases once more to make sure they're as sharp as possible. This creates the tail of your paper airplane.

6. Make the Wings of Your Origami Airplane

Fold the top layer of the paper down to make the first wing of your paper airplane. At the nose, the wing should be slightly above the middle layer of the paper. At the back, it should be slightly above the bottom of the tail you made in the last step.

Repeat the process on the other side to make the second wing of your origami airplane.

7. Fly Your Simple Paper Airplane

Hold your plane at the widest part of the base and gently send it flying across the room! If you're having trouble getting your plane to fly, examine it carefully to make sure it is symmetrical. If one side is even slightly larger than the other, your plane won't fly straight.

Don't worry if you need to make a few practice airplanes before finding a method that works for you. Paper airplanes, just like other forms of origami, take a bit of patience to learn how to make correctly.

Manufactured by Amazon.ca
Bolton, ON